HAL•LEONARD
JAZZ PLAY-ALONG

Book and CD for B♭, E♭, C and Bass Clef Instruments

Volume 125

Arranged and Produced by Mark Taylor

Sammy Nestico

Cover photo © Alamy

ISBN 978-1-4234-9065-4

HAL•LEONARD®
CORPORATION

7777 W. BLUEMOUND RD. P.O. BOX 13819 MILWAUKEE, WI 53213

Visit Hal Leonard Online at
www.halleonard.com

SAMMY NESTICO

Volume 125

Arranged and Produced by Mark Taylor

Featured Players:

Graham Breedlove–Trumpet
John Desalme–Saxes
Tony Nalker–Piano
Jim Roberts–Bass
Chuck Redd–Drums

Recorded at Bias Studios, Springfield, Virginia
Bob Dawson, Engineer

HOW TO USE THE CD:

Each song has <u>two</u> tracks:

1) Split Track/Melody

Woodwind, Brass, Keyboard, and **Mallet Players** can use this track as a learning tool for melody style and inflection.

Bass Players can learn and perform with this track – remove the recorded bass track by turning down the volume on the LEFT channel.

Keyboard and **Guitar Players** can learn and perform with this track – remove the recorded piano part by turning down the volume on the RIGHT channel.

2) Full Stereo Track

Soloists or **Groups** can learn and perform with this accompaniment track with the RHYTHM SECTION only.

FANCY PANTS

BY SAMMY NESTICO

FRECKLE FACE

BY SAMMY NESTICO

C VERSION

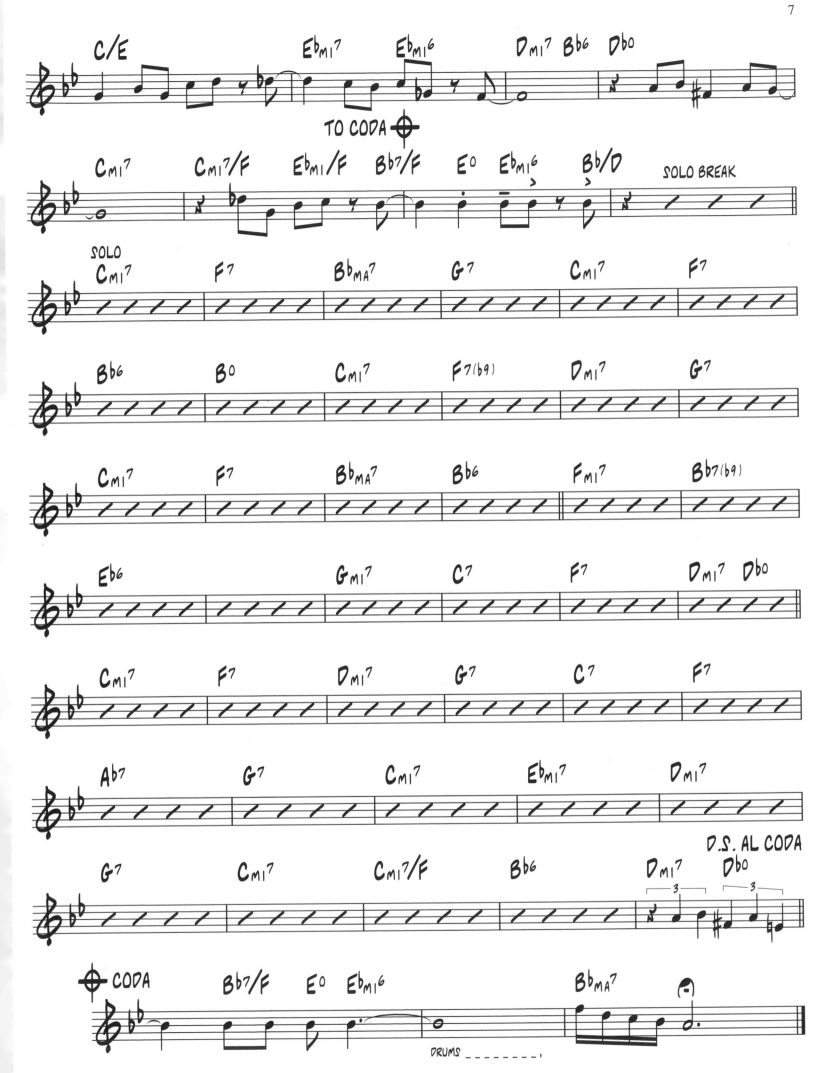

FUN TIME

BY SAMMY NESTICO

C VERSION

MEDIUM SWING

HIGH FIVE

BY SAMMY NESTICO

C VERSION

CD

⓫ : SPLIT TRACK/MELODY
⓬ : FULL STEREO TRACK

C VERSION

THE QUEEN BEE

BY SAMMY NESTICO

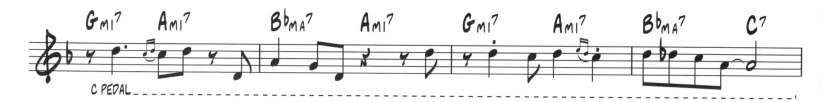

RARE MOMENT

CD
◆13 : SPLIT TRACK/MELODY
◆14 : FULL STEREO TRACK

WORDS BY GARY GRAY
MUSIC BY SAMMY NESTICO

C VERSION

SAMANTHA

WORDS AND MUSIC BY
SAMMY NESTICO

CD
15 : SPLIT TRACK/MELODY
16 : FULL STEREO TRACK

C VERSION

SLOW POP BALLAD

CD

17: SPLIT TRACK/MELODY
18: FULL STEREO TRACK

A WARM BREEZE

BY SAMMY NESTICO

C VERSION

MEDIUM SWING

CD

WIND MACHINE

BY SAMMY NESTICO

C VERSION

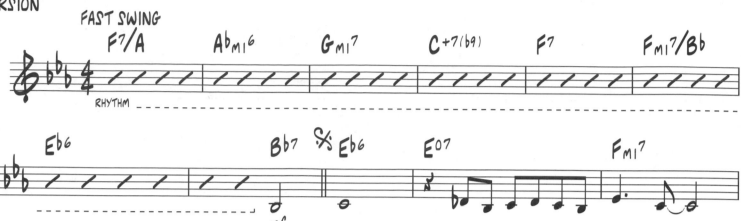

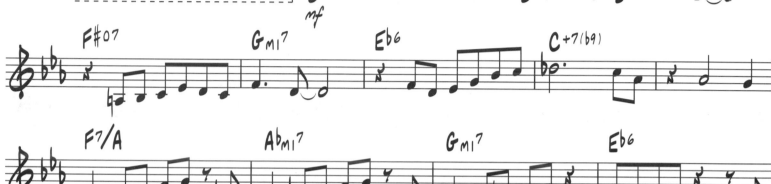

ORCHIDS AND BUTTERFLIES

BY SAMMY NESTICO

C VERSION

ORCHIDS AND BUTTERFLIES

CD
9: SPLIT TRACK/MELODY
10: FULL STEREO TRACK

BY SAMMY NESTICO

Bb VERSION

FANCY PANTS

BY SAMMY NESTICO

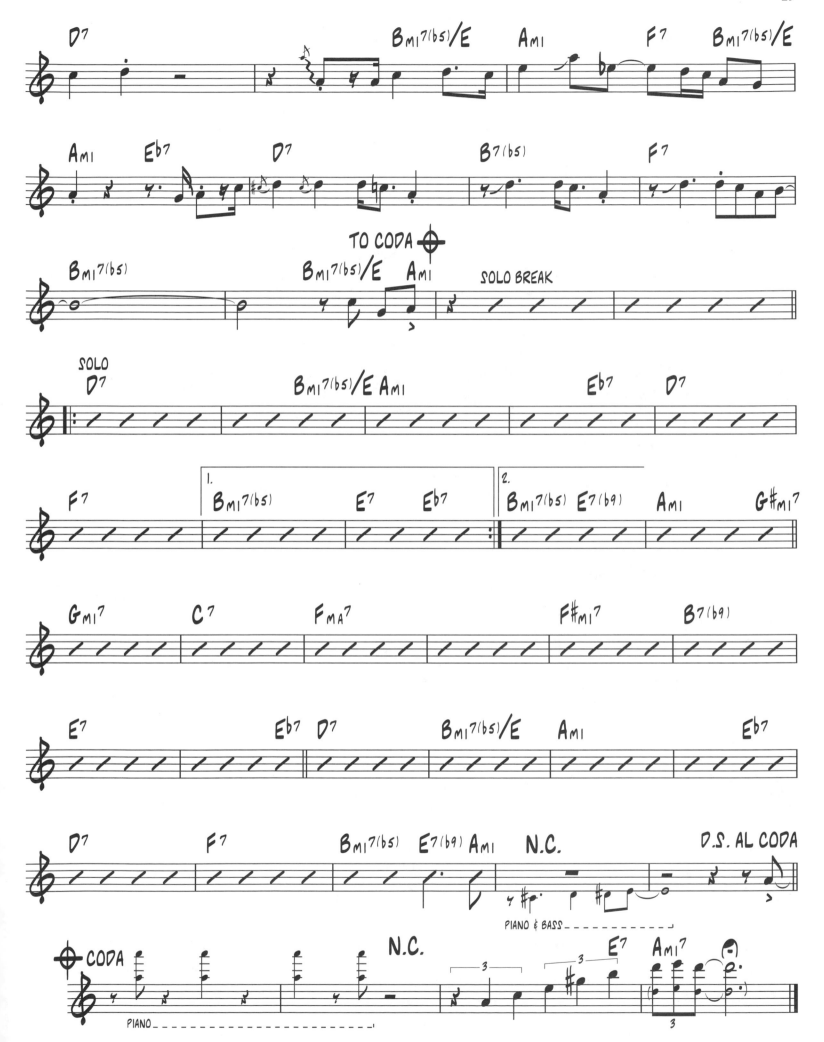

CD
◆3: SPLIT TRACK/MELODY
◆4: FULL STEREO TRACK

FRECKLE FACE

BY SAMMY NESTICO

Bb VERSION

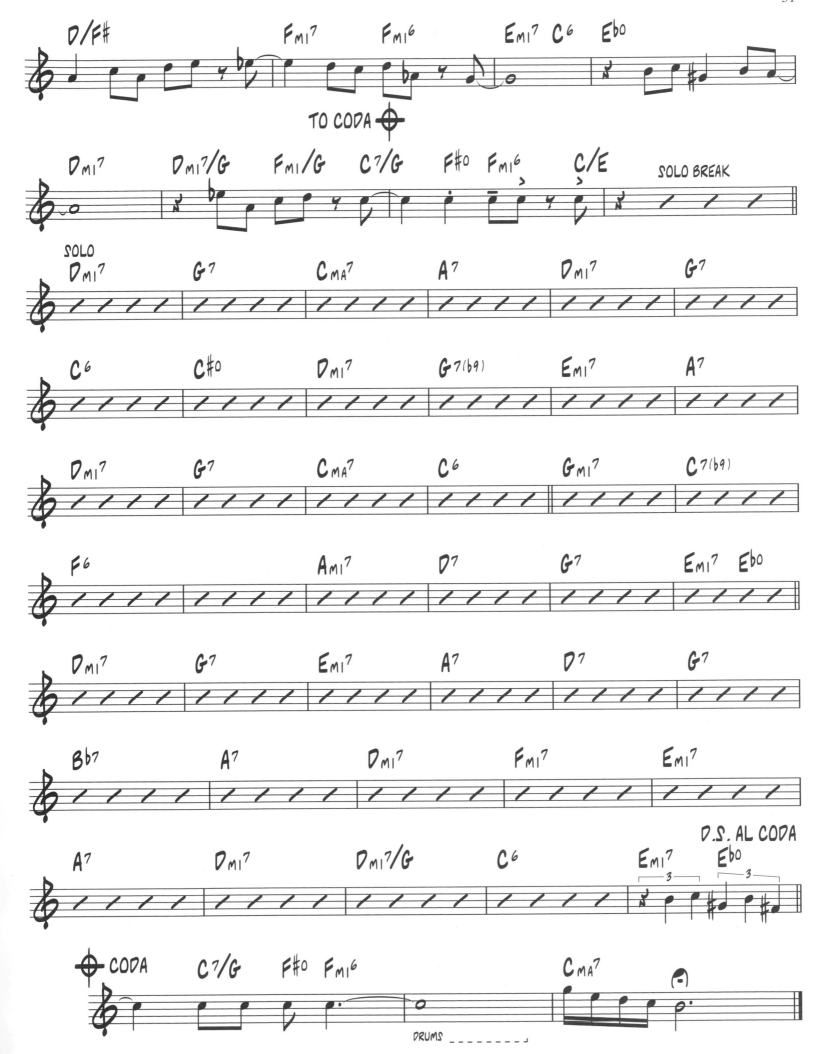

FUN TIME

BY SAMMY NESTICO

CD
5: SPLIT TRACK/MELODY
6: FULL STEREO TRACK

Bb VERSION

33

HIGH FIVE

BY SAMMY NESTICO

CD
7 : SPLIT TRACK/MELODY
8 : FULL STEREO TRACK

Bb VERSION

THE QUEEN BEE

BY SAMMY NESTICO

RARE MOMENT

WORDS BY GARY GRAY
MUSIC BY SAMMY NESTICO

CD
13 : SPLIT TRACK/MELODY
14 : FULL STEREO TRACK

Bb VERSION

CD

Bb VERSION

SAMANTHA

WORDS AND MUSIC BY
SAMMY NESTICO

A Warm Breeze

BY SAMMY NESTICO

Bb VERSION

WIND MACHINE

BY SAMMY NESTICO

Bb VERSION

FAST SWING

FANCY PANTS

BY SAMMY NESTICO

Eb VERSION

Freckle Face

BY SAMMY NESTICO

FUN TIME

BY SAMMY NESTICO

Eb VERSION

High Five

BY SAMMY NESTICO

CD

7 : SPLIT TRACK/MELODY
8 : FULL STEREO TRACK

Eb VERSION

THE QUEEN BEE

BY SAMMY NESTICO

RARE MOMENT

WORDS BY GARY GRAY
MUSIC BY SAMMY NESTICO

Samantha

WORDS AND MUSIC BY
SAMMY NESTICO

Eb VERSION

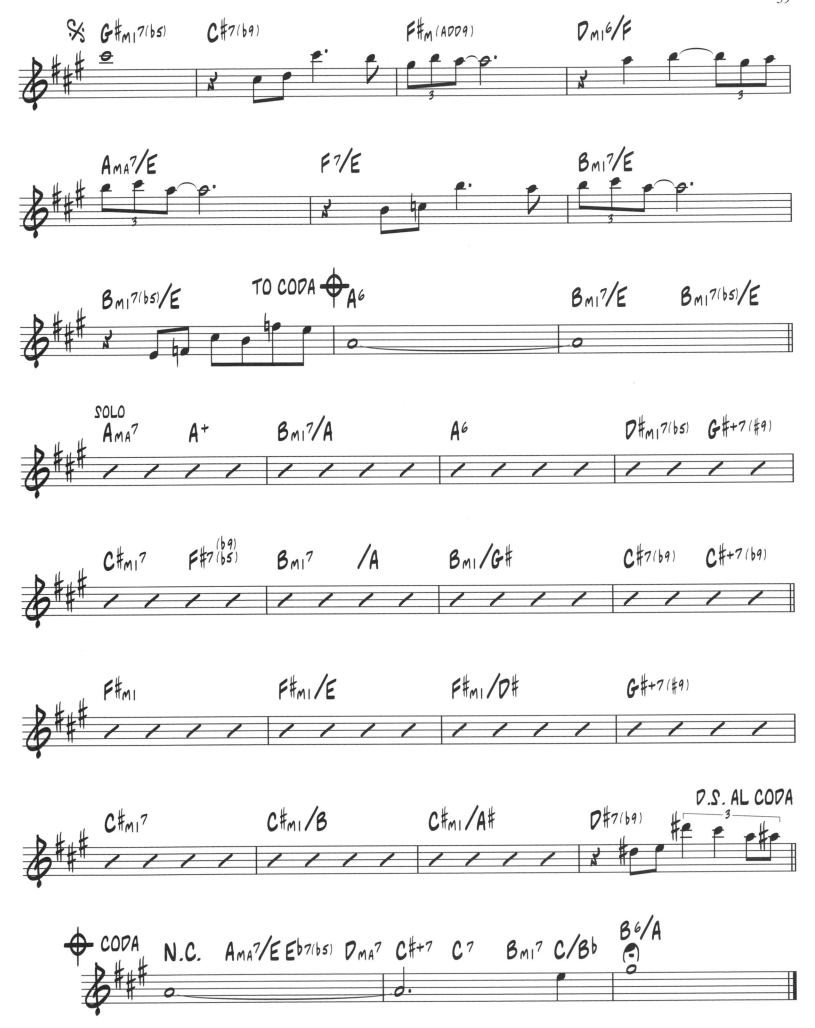

A Warm Breeze

BY SAMMY NESTICO

Eb VERSION

WIND MACHINE

BY SAMMY NESTICO

CD
19 : SPLIT TRACK/MELODY
20 : FULL STEREO TRACK

Eb VERSION

ORCHIDS AND BUTTERFLIES

BY SAMMY NESTICO

Eb VERSION

ORCHIDS AND BUTTERFLIES

By Sammy Nestico

FANCY PANTS

BY SAMMY NESTICO

FRECKLE FACE

BY SAMMY NESTICO

𝄢: C VERSION

FUN TIME

BY SAMMY NESTICO

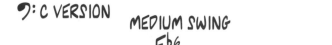

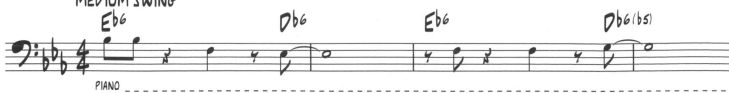

High Five

BY SAMMY NESTICO

 C VERSION

CD

① : SPLIT TRACK/MELODY
② : FULL STEREO TRACK

THE QUEEN BEE

BY SAMMY NESTICO

𝄢: C VERSION

MEDIUM SWING

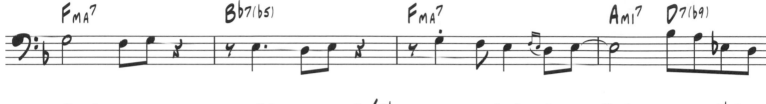

C PEDAL

TO CODA ⊕

CD

RARE MOMENT

WORDS BY GARY GRAY
MUSIC BY SAMMY NESTICO

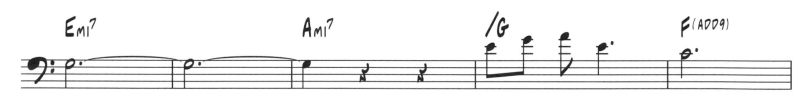

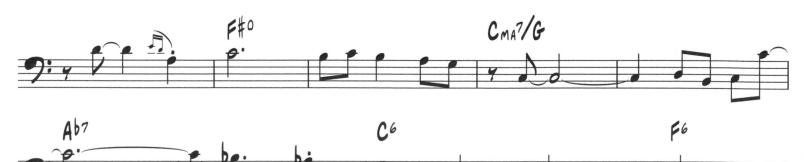

CD

15 : SPLIT TRACK/MELODY
16 : FULL STEREO TRACK

𝄢: C VERSION

SAMANTHA

WORDS AND MUSIC BY
SAMMY NESTICO

SLOW POP BALLAD

A WARM BREEZE

BY SAMMY NESTICO

WIND MACHINE

BY SAMMY NESTICO

Presenting the Hal Leonard JAZZ PLAY-ALONG SERIES

For use with all B-flat, E-flat, Bass Clef and C instruments, the Jazz Play-Along® Series is the ultimate learning tool for all jazz musicians. With musician-friendly lead sheets, melody cues, and other split-track choices on the included CD, these first-of-a-kind packages help you master improvisation while playing some of the greatest tunes of all time. FOR STUDY, each tune includes a split track with: melody cue with proper style and inflection • professional rhythm tracks • choruses for soloing • removable bass part • removable piano part. FOR PERFORMANCE, each tune also has: an additional full stereo accompaniment track (no melody) • additional choruses for soloing.